GW00888649

JANE AUSTEN

Jane Austen was born in 1775 in Steventon, Hampshire, and died in 1817 in Winchester. In her short life she wrote six major novels, *Sense and Sensibility* (1811), *Pride and Prejudice* (1813), *Mansfield Park* (1814), *Emma* (1816), *Northanger Abbey* (1817) and *Persuasion* (1818). She also left two unfinished novels, *The Watsons* and *Sanditon,* as well as *Lady Susan,* a novel unpublished in her lifetime. The three plays in *Young Jane* are based on similarly titled works in Austen's *Juvenilia*, three bound notebooks of stories, letters and plays that she wrote between the ages of twelve and sixteen. The *Juvenilia* remained unpublished for more than a hundred years after her death.

CECILY O'NEILL

Cecily O'Neill is the founder and director of **2TimeTheatre**. She works extensively with playwrights, actors, teachers and students and is the author of several influential books on drama education. Previous adaptations include *Venus and Adonis* (Winchester Festival 2016), *Drinking with Dorothy* (Players Theatre, New York 2015) and *The Golden Apple* (Dublin Theatre Festival 2008).

YOUNG JANE

By

Cecily O'Neill

Three Plays

Inspired by

JANE AUSTEN'S

JUVENILIA

First published in the UK in 2016 by

2TimeTheatre
56 Marston Gate
Winchester SO23 7DS, UK

www.2timetheatre.com

Cover design by Tracey Winwood
Printed by Sarsen Press, 22 Hyde Street, Winchester SO23 7DR

Copyright © Cecily O'Neill 2016

All rights whatsoever in this play are strictly reserved. No part of this book may be reproduced or transmitted in any form or by any means, electronic or mechanical, including photocopying, recording or by any information-and-retrieval system, without written permission from the copyright holder and 2TimeTheatre.

All enquiries concerning performance rights, readings, excerpts or any other use of these plays by amateurs or professionals should be applied for in advance to: 2timetheatre@gmail.com

ISBN: 978-0-9955468-0-6

CONTENTS

INTRODUCTION

Jane Austen (1775 - 1817) is one of the most popular and acclaimed novelists in English literature. Her six major novels are *Sense and Sensibility*, *Pride and Prejudice*, *Mansfield Park*, *Emma*, *Northanger Abbey* and *Persuasion*.

Jane Austen was born in December 1775 in the village of Steventon near Basingstoke in Hampshire, where her father was Rector and where she spent the first twenty-six years of her life. The busy household included five of her six brothers and her beloved sister Cassandra, as well as a number of boys who were tutored by her father and lived with the family. Her brother George had a mental or physical impairment and was cared for elsewhere.

Like the rest of her family, Jane was an avid reader. She had access to her father's large library as well as to the books available in the local circulating library. Her favourite authors included Fielding, Fanny Burney, Mrs Radcliffe and Samuel Richardson.

Music was also a favourite diversion and Jane was an excellent musician, like a number of the characters in her novels. In *Pride and Prejudice*, Elizabeth Bennet, the Bingley sisters and Georgiana Darcy are accomplished pianists. Jane practised for several hours every morning on the Steventon piano before the rest of the family was awake. She also studied for several years with Dr Chard, an organist at Winchester Cathedral. The family ordered the latest sheet music from London and it was carefully copied by hand into personal albums.

As Jane grew up in the pleasant Hampshire countryside perhaps reading and music weren't her only pleasures. One of Austen's youngest and most delightful characters is Catherine Morland, the heroine of *Northanger Abbey*, whose favourite activities are described so vividly that it is easy to believe Jane herself delighted in similar pastimes, growing up as she did in a house full of boys. Catherine Morland prefers

> *cricket, baseball, riding on horseback, and running about the country to books... provided they were all story and no reflection, she had never any objection to books at all... .*

Austen had another more significant pastime. From a very early age she wrote poems, stories and plays for the amusement of her friends and family. Between 1788 when Jane was twelve and 1792 when she was sixteen, she copied many of these pieces into three bound notebooks, now known as the *Juvenilia*. These volumes include a number of short novels, usually written as a series of letters and often left unfinished. There are also several short dramas and many other fragments. Almost all of these pieces are introduced by a grandiose dedication to a member of the family.

Jane's father certainly encouraged her to think of herself as a writer. He gave her two of the *Juvenilia* notebooks and inside the cover of the third notebook he wrote '*Effusions of Fancy by a Very Young Lady consisting of Tales in a Style entirely new*'. Her portable writing desk is believed to have been a gift from him. And although the attempt was unsuccessful, in 1797 he approached a London publisher with *First Impressions* - '*a manuscript novel in three volumes*' which was later to appear as *Pride and Prejudice*.

Among the surprising aspects of Austen's teenage efforts is her display of a considerable literary technique and a firm understanding of different conventions and genres. She particularly delights in ridiculing the improbable events and extravagant sentiments of the popular novels of the time. A favourite practice is to condense the events of the story and to exaggerate both the happiness and misfortunes of the characters, contrasting their calculating callousness with their expressions of lofty sensibility. The exuberance, absurdity and moral anarchy of her early fictions and the frequent drunkenness, illegitimacy and immorality of her characters may surprise admirers of Austen's mature novels.

In 1869 James Edward Leigh-Austen, Austen's nephew and her first biographer, gave his opinion of what he called *'her early childhood effusions'*.

Her earliest stories are of a slight and flimsy texture, and are generally intended to be nonsensical, but the nonsense has much spirit in it. They are usually preceded by a dedication of mock solemnity to some one of her family. They are always composed in pure simple English, quite free from the over-ornamented style which might be expected from so young a writer.

An example of Austen's early style comes from a *Letter from a Young Lady* included in *Volume the Second* of the *Juvenilia*.

My beloved Ellinor

Many have been the troubles of my past life and the only consolation I feel is that I am convinced that I have strictly deserved them. I murdered my Father at a very early period of my life. I have since murdered my Mother, and I am now going to murder my Sister. I have changed my religion so often that at present I have no idea of any religion left. I have been a perjured witness in every public trial for the last twelve years; and I have forged my own Will. In short, there is scarcely a crime that I have not committed – But I am now going to reform...

Volume the First of the *Juvenilia* begins with *Jack and Alice*, a novel dedicated to Jane's brother Francis, a midshipman. He must have enjoyed reading about the 54ᵗʰ birthday party of Mr. Johnson. The guests included Charles Adams, *'who was an amiable, accomplished and bewitching young man, of so dazzling a beauty that none but eagles could look him in the face'*. The eldest Miss Simpson was *'pleasing in her person, in her manners and her disposition and an unbounded ambition was her only fault'*. Her sister Sukey was *'envious, spiteful and malicious'* and Cecilia, the youngest sister, *'was perfectly handsome but too affected to be pleasing'*.

Austen may have been as young as twelve when she wrote these character sketches, with their mixture of exact description and comic exaggeration. In 1800, at the age of twenty-five, Austen wrote to Cassandra about her attendance at a local ball. Her impressions of the people she meets are sharp and concise and reminiscent of her earlier descriptions.

> *There were very few beauties and such as there were, were not very handsome... Mrs. Blount was the only one much admired... with the same broad face, diamond bandeau, white shoes, pink husband and fat neck.*

In Bath she noticed a Miss Langley *'like any other short girl, with a broad nose and wide mouth, fashionable dress and exposed bosom'*, and Admiral Stanhope, *'a gentlemanlike man, but his legs are too short and his tail too long...'*.

The young Jane Austen was clearly a keen observer of the faults and failings of the people she encountered in life and literature. The three volumes of the *Juvenilia* display her sharp insight into character, her savage wit and her skill in dialogue, already foreshadowing the extraordinary writer she was to become. The mocking and occasionally brutal tone of her teenage writing is rare in her later work but occasional echoes remain in her letters. In October 1798 she wrote to her sister Cassandra,

> *Mrs. Hall of Sherborne was brought to bed yesterday of a dead child, some weeks before she expected, owing to a fright. I suppose she happened unawares to look at her husband.*

Austen's capacity to capture a character's foibles and absurdities in a few sentences is a key feature of her mature novels. Mr. Collins, Lady Catherine, Mrs. Norris and Mrs. Elton immediately reveal themselves through what they say and it is Elizabeth Bennet's lively wit and sympathetic responses that have made her such a beloved character. But Austen was already a master of dialogue in her teenage work.

In one of the letters from *Volume the Second* of the *Juvenilia*, a certain Lady Greville is surprised to discover that her daughter's friend Maria, who is in '*distressed circumstances*', is wearing a new dress. Lady Greville feels free to comment on it.

> '*So Miss Maria…have you got a new gown on?*' *(feeling the fabric)*. '*I dare say it is all very smart. But I must own, for*

you know I always speak my mind, that I think it was quite a needless piece of expense. Why could not you have worn your old striped gown? It is not my way to find fault with people because they are poor, for I always think that they are more to be despised and pitied than blamed for it, especially if they can't help it, but at the same time I must say that in my opinion your old striped gown would have been quite fine enough for you. To tell you the truth - I always speak my mind - I am very much afraid that half the people in the room will not know whether you have a gown on or not.'

Lady Greville's speech clearly anticipates the snobbery, ill breeding and impertinence of Lady Catherine de Burgh in *Pride and Prejudice*.

In 1809, after some unsettled years in Bath and Southampton, Jane Austen, with her mother, sister Cassandra and their friend Martha Lloyd, moved to Chawton in Hampshire, a village close to their old home in Steventon. Their new home was part of the Chawton estate, which belonged to Jane's brother, Edward Knight, and is now the Jane Austen's House Museum.

These were Austen's most productive years and four of her novels – *Sense and Sensibility*, *Pride and Prejudice*, *Mansfield Park* and *Emma* – were published between 1811 and 1816. At last she had begun to find real success as a writer.

Austen's health had been declining for several years and in May 1817 she moved to Winchester to receive medical treatment. She died there in July 1817 and was buried in Winchester Cathedral. She was forty-two years old. *Northanger Abbey* and *Persuasion* were published posthumously. Her last novel, *Sanditon*, remained unfinished.

Her great admirer Rudyard Kipling wrote,

Jane lies in Winchester — blessed be her shade!
Praise the Lord for making her, and her for all she made!
And while the stones of Winchester or Milsom Street remain,
Glory, love and honour unto England's Jane.

YOUNG JANE

Prologue

The Three Sisters

The Visit

Love and Friendship

PROLOGUE

Characters

REV. AUSTEN
MRS AUSTEN
JAMES
EDWARD
HENRY
FRANK
CHARLES
GEORGE
CASSANDRA
JANE

Music. The cast assembles on stage, creating a family tableau – the REV. AUSTEN *and* MRS AUSTEN *surrounded by their children.* MRS AUSTEN *is holding a baby.*

REV. AUSTEN   1775. A hard winter. On December 16th my daughter Jane was born. The child came in the evening without much warning and everything was happily soon over.

MRS AUSTEN   She will be a present plaything and a future companion for her sister Cassandra. *(She hands the baby to* CASSANDRA.*)*

JAMES   And James!

EDWARD   And Edward!

HENRY   And Henry!

FRANK   And Frank!

CHARLES   And Charles!

GEORGE   And George!

ALL   Poor George!

GEORGE *exits sadly.*

CASSANDRA   Jane will be the sun of my life, the gilder of every pleasure, the soother of every sorrow.

CASSANDRA *leaves with the baby but returns almost immediately and hands out books to the others.*

REV. AUSTEN   We are a reading family. My library contains over 500 books.

The family settles down with books.

JAMES   The Spectator.

HENRY   The Tatler.

EDWARD   William Cowper.

CHARLES   Dr. Johnson.

FRANK   Henry Fielding.

CASSANDRA   Maria Edgeworth.

JANE *enters with a book and a notebook.*

JANE   And Mrs Radcliffe and Fanny Burney and
Charlotte Smith and Samuel Richardson!

MRS AUSTEN   And there's always the circulating
library. We are all great novel-readers, and not
ashamed of being so.

HENRY   And we love our family theatricals!

ALL   At Christmas – in the barn!

FRANK   *The Rivals!*

EDWARD   *Tom Thumb!*

CHARLES   *The Wonder!*

HENRY   *Which is the Man!*

JAMES   I provide the prologues and epilogues for all our productions because I am the writer of the family. At Oxford my magazine *The Loiterer* had five editions.

ALL *(admiringly)*   *The Loiterer!* Five Editions!

They pass around a journal, which ends up in JANE's *hands.*

JANE   It's very fine, James, but *The Loiterer* takes no notice of its female readers. Let us have some nice affecting stories. Let the lover be killed in a duel, or lost at sea, or you may make him shoot himself, just as you please. And his mistress will of course run mad. Only remember that the lovers must have very pretty names.

REV. AUSTEN   Is that how you mean to write, my dear? (*He takes* JANE's *notebook and reads aloud.*) 'Effusions of Fancy by a Very Young Lady consisting of Tales in a Style entirely new.'

The others take the notebook and pass it around, reading the titles aloud.

JAMES   'Frederic and Elfrida!'

GEORGE   'Jack and Alice!'

EDWARD   'Edgar and Emma!'

HENRY   'Henry and Eliza!'

CASSANDRA   'The Beautiful Cassandra!'

FRANK   'The Visit!'

CHARLES   'The Mystery!'

MRS AUSTEN   'Love and Friendship!'

REV. AUSTEN   'The Three Sisters.' I would like to hear it, but we have only two sisters.

MRS AUSTEN   Never fear, my dear. We'll manage it between us!

REV. AUSTEN   Well, let us see what you can do!

Music.

THE THREE SISTERS

Characters

MARY STANHOPE
MRS STANHOPE, her mother
GEORGIANA, her sister
SOPHY, her sister
MR WATTS, her suitor

Mrs Stanhope's parlour, sometime in the 1790s.

MARY STANHOPE, *a girl of about 18, enters. She holds a letter and speaks directly to the audience.*

MARY   I am the happiest creature in the world! I have received an offer of marriage from Mr Watts! It is the first proposal I have ever had, but I do not intend to accept it. At least I believe I won't. Mr Watts is quite an old man, at least thirty-two. He's very plain - so plain that I cannot bear to look at him. He's also extremely disagreeable and I hate him more than anybody else in the world! He has a large fortune but then he's so very healthy. I don't know what to do! If I refuse him, he said he'd offer himself to Sophy and if she refused him, to Georgiana, and I can't bear to have either of my

15

sisters married before me. But if I accept him, I know I'll be miserable for the rest of my life. He's very ill-tempered and extremely jealous and stingy!

MRS STANHOPE (*offstage*) Mary! Mary, my dear! Mr Watts has arrived!

MARY He's here! He told me he meant to speak to Mama today. I declare I won't see him. She will probably make me marry him whether I will or not. But I believe I'll accept him. It will be such a triumph to be married before Sophy and Georgiana and Kitty Dutton! And he promised to have a new carriage when we marry - but we almost quarrelled about the colour. I want it to be blue spotted with silver, and he insisted it should be a plain chocolate!

MRS STANHOPE (*offstage*) Mary!

MARY He said he would come today and take my final answer, so I believe I must get him while I can. Kitty Dutton will envy me and I'll be able to chaperone Sophy and Georgiana and the Duttons to all the Winter Balls. But what will be the use of that when he probably won't let me go myself! I know he hates dancing and he talks a great deal of the importance of women always staying at home and such rubbish. I would refuse him at once if I were certain that neither of my sisters would accept him. But then he might propose to Kitty.... No, I can't run such a risk. If he'll promise to have the carriage painted as I like, I'll have him. If not, he may ride in it by himself!

MRS STANHOPE *enters.*

MRS STANHOPE   Mary, I want to speak to you on a very particular subject.

MARY   I know what you mean. That fool Mr Watts has told you all about it. You shan't force me to have him if I don't want to.

MRS STANHOPE   I am not going to force you, child. I only want to insist upon your making up your mind one way or the other. If you don't accept him, Sophy may.

MARY   Sophy needn't trouble herself, for I shall certainly marry him myself.

MRS STANHOPE   Then why should you be afraid of my forcing your inclinations?

MARY   Why? Because I have not settled whether I shall have him or not.

MRS STANHOPE   You are the strangest girl in the world, Mary. What you say one moment, you unsay the next. Tell me whether or not you intend to marry Mr Watts!

MARY   Lord, Mama, how can I tell you what I don't know myself?

MRS STANHOPE   Then I desire you will know, and quickly too, for Mr Watts says he won't be kept in suspense.

MARY   That depends upon me.

MRS STANHOPE   No, it does not, for if you don't give him your final answer today he intends to pay his addresses to Sophy.

MARY   Then I shall tell the world that he behaved very ill to me.

MRS STANHOPE   What good will that do? Mr Watts has been too long abused by the world to mind it now.

MARY   I wish I had a father or a brother who could fight him.

MRS STANHOPE   Mr Watts would run away first! You must decide today either to accept or refuse him.

MARY   But if I won't have him, why must he ask my sisters?

MRS STANHOPE   Why? Because he wishes to be allied to the family and because they are just as pretty as you.

MARY   But will Sophy marry him if he asks her?

MRS STANHOPE   Why shouldn't she? But if she won't, then Georgiana must. I am determined not to miss this opportunity of settling one of my daughters so well.   So make the most of your time. I leave you to settle the matter with yourself.

MRS STANHOPE *exits.*

MARY   I know! I'll ask Sophy and Georgiana if they'd marry him and if they say they won't, I'll refuse him too, for I hate him more than you can imagine. As for the Duttons, if he marries one of them, at least I shall have the triumph of refusing him first.

MARY *exits as* GEORGIANA *and* SOPHY *enter.*

GEORGIANA   Mary seems to have a particular dislike of Mr Watts, yet she means to marry him rather than risk his offering marriage to us. The silly girl considers our marrying before her as one of the greatest misfortunes that could possibly befall. She'd willingly risk everlasting misery with Mr Watts in order to prevent it. Mama insists she will not allow him to look any farther than our own family for a wife. So if Mary refuses him, and you won't take him, Mama has resolved that I must.

SOPHY   Poor Georgiana!

GEORGIANA   Our mother's resolutions are always strictly kept, but I shan't expect you to sacrifice your happiness on my account by becoming his wife.

SOPHY   Never fear. Mary won't refuse him. I believe that she likes him more than she will admit. Yet how can I hope that my sister will accept a man who may not make her happy?

GEORGIANA   He may not make her happy but his fortune, his name, his house, and his carriage will. I am sure that Mary will marry him - indeed why shouldn't she? He is not more than thirty-two - a very proper age for a man to marry at. He is rather plain to be sure, but then what is beauty in a man if he has a genteel figure and a sensible looking face?

SOPHY (*laughing*)   True, Georgiana, but Mr Watts' figure is unfortunately extremely vulgar and his countenance is very heavy. He seems ill-tempered – but perhaps that is just **an open frankness which becomes a man.** And we know that Mary is not known for the sweetness of her temper. They say he is stingy – let's call that prudence. They say he is jealous, but that may proceed from the warmth of his heart. But I see no reason why he shouldn't make a very good husband, or why Mary shouldn't be very happy with him.

GEORGIANA   Whether she accepts him or not, I would not marry Mr Watts if beggary was the only alternative. He is so deficient in every respect! Hideous in his person and without one good quality to make amends for it! To be sure his fortune is good. But it is not so very large! Three thousand a year - what is three thousand a year? It will not tempt me.

SOPHY   How much would you settle for, Georgiana, if another such gentleman came calling?

GEORGIANA   Such a one as Mr Watts? Ten thousand a year might tempt me.

SOPHY I should like a little love and respect into the bargain. But remember that three thousand a year is six times our mother's income. Mary will enjoy being a married woman and it will be a noble fortune for her.

GEORGIANA For Mary! It will give me pleasure to see her in such affluence. Here she comes. She seems to be in some agitation.

MARY *enters.*

MARY Pray, Sophy, have you any mind to be married?

SOPHY To be married! Not in the least. But why do you ask me? Do you know someone who means to make me a proposal?

MARY No, how should I? But mayn't I ask a common question?

GEORGIANA Not a very common one, surely.

MARY Would you like to marry Mr Watts, Sophy?

GEORGIANA Why should she not? Who would not rejoice to marry a man of three thousand a year? If he dies there will be a noble jointure.

MARY But would you marry him, Sophy?

SOPHY I should certainly act as Georgiana would.

MARY Well then, I've had an offer from Mr Watts!

GEORGIANA (*pretending surprise*) Oh, pray don't accept him, Mary, and then he may ask me!

MARY Would you believe it, Sophy, the fool wants to have his new carriage just the same colour as the old one. And if he won't let it be blue spotted with silver, I won't have him. Oh, here he comes! I know he'll be rude. I know he'll be ill-tempered and won't say one civil thing to me - or behave at all like a lover.

MR WATTS *enters with* MRS STANHOPE.

WATTS (*bowing*) Ladies, your most obedient servant. Fine weather, ladies. (*To* MARY) Well, Miss Stanhope, I hope you have at last settled the matter in your own mind and will be so good as to let me know whether you will condescend to marry me or not.

MARY I think, Sir, you might have asked me in a genteeler way than that. I do not know whether I shall have you if you behave so odd.

MRS STANHOPE Mary!

MARY Well, Mama, if he will be so cross...

MRS STANHOPE Hush, hush, Mary, you shall not be rude to Mr Watts.

WATTS Pray, Madam, do not oblige Miss Stanhope to be polite. If she does not choose to accept my hand, I can offer it elsewhere, for I have no particular preference to you above your sisters. It is the same to me which of the three I marry.

MARY   Well then, I will have you if I must.

WATTS   I should have thought, Miss Stanhope, when such settlements are offered there can be no great violence done to your inclinations in accepting them.

MARY (*aside*)   What's the use of a great jointure if men will live forever? (*To* WATTS) Remember the pin money - two hundred a year.

WATTS   A hundred and seventy-five, Madam.

MRS STANHOPE   Two hundred indeed, Sir.

MARY   And remember I am to have a new carriage blue spotted with silver; and I shall expect a new saddle horse, a suit of fine lace, and an infinite number of the most valuable jewels. You must set up your carriage which must be cream coloured, and you must drive me out in it every day. You must hire two more footmen to attend me, two women to wait on me, and you must always let me do just as I please – oh, and you must make a very good husband.

MRS STANHOPE   This is all very reasonable for my daughter to expect.

WATTS   And it is very reasonable that your daughter should be disappointed, Mrs Stanhope.

MARY (*warming to her theme*)   You must let me spend every winter in Bath, every spring in town, every summer taking some tour, and every autumn at a watering place, and if we are at home the rest of the year, you must do nothing but give balls and masquerades. You must build a theatre to act plays in. I know! The first play we give shall be *Which is the Man*, and I will play Lady Bell Bloomer!

WATTS   And pray, Miss Stanhope, what am I to expect from you in return for all this?

MARY   Expect? Why, you may expect to have me pleased.

WATTS   It would be odd if you were not. Your expectations, Madam, are too high for me, and I must apply to Miss Sophy, who perhaps may not have raised hers so much.

SOPHY   You are mistaken, Sir. Though they may not be exactly in the same line, my expectations are as high as my sister's. I expect my husband to be good tempered and cheerful, to consult my happiness in all his actions, and to love me with constancy and sincerity.

WATTS   These are very odd ideas, young lady. You had better discard them before you marry, or you will be obliged to do so afterwards.

MARY (*hurriedly apologizing*)   You are mistaken Mr Watts if you think I was in earnest when I said I expected so much. However I must have a new carriage.

MRS STANHOPE Yes Sir, you must allow that. Mary has a right to expect that.

WATTS I have always meant to have a new one on my marriage, Mrs Stanhope. But it shall be the colour of my present one.

MRS STANHOPE I think, Mr Watts, you should pay my girl the compliment of consulting her taste on such matters.

SOPHY Perhaps, to please you, Mr Watts, the carriage could be a dark brown, and to please you, Mary, it might have a silver border.

MRS STANHOPE An excellent suggestion, Sophy. Come, shake hands on it.

WATTS *and* MARY *shake hands reluctantly.*

WATTS I hope you are satisfied, madam. As to the rest, you will have all the family jewels and I promise to buy you a saddle horse; but in return you are not to expect to go to town or any other public place for these three years. There will be neither theatre nor masquerades; and you must be contented with one maid.

MARY But...

MRS STANHOPE Hush, child! Now these matters are settled so happily, let us examine the settlement papers in the next room, Mr Watts.

WATTS *and* MRS STANHOPE *exit.*

MARY   Thank Heaven! He's gone at last. How I hate him!

SOPHY   My dear Mary! It shows great impropriety to say that you dislike the man who will be your husband.

MARY   I declare I do hate him! I hope I never see him again!

SOPHY   Can you not like him a little, Mary? I think you do.

MARY   Perhaps I don't dislike him so very much, though he is very plain to be sure. But I believe Mr Watts must be very much in love with me, so it will be quite a match of affection on his side.

SOPHY   Not only on his, I hope.

MARY   Oh! When there is love on one side, there is no occasion for it on the other. Do you think it will be necessary to have all the jewels new set?

GEORGIANA   Necessary for what?

MARY   For what? Why, for my appearance at the next Ball after I am married. I shall be happy to chaperone both of you.

GEORGIANA   Well, if you are inclined to undertake the care of young ladies, you should ask Mrs Edgecumbe to let you chaperone her six daughters, which, with ourselves and Kitty Dutton, will make your Entrée to the Ball very impressive.

MARY No, I shouldn't like to chaperone so many.

SOPHY Look, I think he's coming a-courting again, in a true lover like manner.

MARY You need not have told me that. I know very well why he's come.

WATTS *enters.*

WATTS So, Madam, all is agreed, and I leave for London to obtain the Licence.

MARY Do as you please, Sir. Do not hurry on my account.

WATTS Madam, you are not civil!

MARY I can't wait to visit London. There must be many men there much handsomer than you!

WATTS Madam, you are a vixen!

MARY And you are a blackguard, Sir!

WATTS Farewell!

WATTS *exits in a fury.*

MARY Mr Watts is such a fool! I hope I never see him again.

SOPHY But Mary, he is leaving. How will you make up your quarrel?

MARY He ought to ask my pardon; but even if he does, I won't forgive him.

GEORGIANA   His submission won't be very useful, then.

MRS STANHOPE *enters.*

MRS STANHOPE   Mary, what were you thinking! Mr Watts has been complaining to me of your behaviour. But I have finally persuaded him to think no more of it. Mr Watts is going to town to hasten the preparations for the wedding. It cannot happen too soon, before you both quarrel again. Come and bid him farewell.

MARY   But Mama...

MRS STANHOPE   At once, Mary!

MARY *and* MRS STANHOPE *exit.*

GEORGIANA   What a wedding that will be!

SOPHY   And what a marriage – based on little esteem and less understanding!

GEORGIANA   And think of the children – with his appearance, Mary's wit, and ill temper on both sides!

SOPHY   Marriage is a great improver. Perhaps time will sooth their tempers and ease their discontents.

GEORGIANA   If we marry let us take care to be more careful in our choice of husbands!

SOPHY   I'm afraid we must marry if we can. But I would rather be a teacher in a school than marry a man I did not like. Anything is to be endured rather than marrying without affection.

GEORGIANA   A teacher! I can think of nothing worse!

SOPHY   And are we not told that marriage is the highest kind of friendship we can ever know?

GEORGIANA   Alas, how few ever reach that happy state!

SOPHY   True affection and respect on both sides would make a good beginning.

GEORGIANA   And the addition of money and position might ensure a happy ending!

SOPHY   Let us wish Mary such an ending with all our hearts!

Music.

YOUNG JANE

THE VISIT

Characters

LORD FITZGERALD
MISS FITZGERALD, his sister
MR STANLY, his cousin
SIR ARTHUR HAMPTON
LADY HAMPTON
SOPHY HAMPTON, their daughter
MR WILLOUGHBY, Sir Arthur's nephew
CHLOE WILLOUGHBY, his sister
SERVANT

Lord Fitzgerald's dining-parlour sometime in the 1790's.

LORD FITZGERALD *and* MISS FITZGERALD *enter stage right.* STANLY *enters stage left.*

STANLY   Cousin, your servant.

FITZGERALD   Stanly, good morning to you. I hope you slept well.

STANLY (*in obvious discomfort*)   Remarkably well, thank you.

FITZGERALD   I am afraid you found your bed too short. This was my Grandmother's house and all the beds were bought in her time. She was a very short woman and made a point of suiting all her beds to her own length, as she never wished to have any company in the house.

STANLY   Make no more excuses, dear Fitzgerald.

FITZGERALD   I will not distress you by too much civility – I only beg you will consider yourself as much at home here as in your father's house. Remember the saying, 'The more free, the more welcome'.

STANLY   Thanks, cousin. What company do you expect to dine with us today?

MISS FITZGERALD   Sir Arthur and Lady Hampton. Their daughter, Sophy. Their nephew, Willoughby and their niece, Chloe. Brother, I believe I hear their carriage.

FITZGERALD   If you will excuse me, I will receive them myself. My Grandmother's servants are poorly trained and unused to company.

LORD FITZGERALD *exits.*

STANLY   Miss Hampton and her cousin are both very handsome, are they not?

MISS FITZGERALD   Miss Chloe Willoughby is
   extremely handsome. Miss Sophy Hampton is a fine
   girl but not her equal.

STANLY   Is not your brother much attached to Miss
   Hampton?

MISS FITZGERALD   He admires her, I know, but I
   believe there is nothing more in it. I have heard him
   say that Sophy was the most beautiful, pleasing and
   amiable girl in the whole world and that of all
   others he should prefer her for his wife, but I am
   certain it never went any farther.

STANLY   And yet my cousin never says a thing he does
   not mean.

MISS FITZGERALD   Never. From his cradle he has
   always been a strict adherent to truth. He never told
   a lie but once, and that was to oblige me. There
   never was such a brother!

LORD FITZGERALD *enters.*

FITZGERALD   Our guests have arrived!

The SERVANT *enters and announces the* GUESTS *who enter
as their names are called.*

SERVANT   Sir Arthur and Lady Hampton. Miss
   Hampton. Mr and Miss Willoughby.

MISS FITZGERALD (*to* LADY HAMPTON)   I hope
   I have the pleasure of seeing your Ladyship well -

(*to* SIR ARTHUR) Sir Arthur, your servant. (*to* WILLOUGHBY) Yours, Mr Willoughby. (*to the girls*) Dear Sophy. Dear Chloe.

The GUESTS *bow and curtsey.*

Pray be seated everyone. Bless me! There ought to be eight chairs and there are only six. However, if your Ladyship will take Sir Arthur in your lap, and if Sophy will take my brother in hers, I believe we shall do pretty well.

LADY HAMPTON   Oh, with pleasure.

SIR ARTHUR *sits on* LADY HAMPTON'S *knee.*

SOPHY   I beg his Lordship will be seated.

LORD FITZGERALD *sits on* SOPHY'S *knee.*

MISS FITZGERALD   I am really shocked at crowding you in such a manner, but my Grandmother disliked company, and did not think it necessary to buy more chairs than were sufficient for her own family.

SOPHY   Make no apologies, Miss Fitzgerald. Your brother is very light.

STANLY (*aside*)   What a cherub is Chloe!

CHLOE (*aside*)   What a seraph is Stanly!

THE SERVANT *enters with various dishes.*

SERVANT   Dinner is served! (*He names each dish as it is placed on the table.*) Fried cowheel and onions. Red herrings. Tripe. Liver and crow.

CHLOE (*coyly*)   May I trouble Mr Stanly for a little fried cow heel and onion?

STANLY   Oh Madam, there is a secret pleasure in helping so amiable a lady.

FITZGERALD   Some wine, Sir Arthur?

SIR ARTHUR *attempts to accept everything that is offered to him, without success.*

LADY HAMPTON   I assure you, my Lord, Sir Arthur never touches wine; but I am sure Sophy will toss off a bumper to oblige you.

FITZGERALD   Elder wine or mead, Miss Hampton?

SOPHY   If it is the same to you, Sir, I should prefer some warm ale with a toast and nutmeg.

FITZGERALD (*to* SERVANT)   Two glasses of warmed ale with a toast and nutmeg.

The SERVANT *presents them with the ale. As the meal proceeds, everyone gradually becomes tipsy.*

MISS FITZGERALD (*flirtatiously*)   I am afraid, Mr Willoughby, you take no care of yourself. I fear you don't meet with anything to your liking.

WILLOUGHBY Oh! Madam, I can want for nothing while there are red herrings on the table!

FITZGERALD Sir Arthur, taste that tripe. I think you will find it good.

LADY HAMPTON Sir Arthur never eats tripe. It is too savoury for him, my Lord.

MISS FITZGERALD (*to the* SERVANT) Take away the liver and crow, and bring in the suet pudding.

The SERVANT *clears the table and prepares to serve the pudding.*

MISS FITZGERALD Sir Arthur, shan't I send you a bit of pudding?

LADY HAMPTON Sir Arthur never eats suet pudding, Ma'am. It is too high a dish for him.

MISS FITZGERALD Will no one allow me the honour of helping them? Then take away the pudding, and bring the wine.

The SERVANT *brings in the wine.*

FITZGERALD I wish we had any dessert to offer you. But my Grandmother destroyed the hothouse in order to build a receptacle for the turkeys.

LADY HAMPTON I beg you will make no apologies, my Lord.

WILLOUGHBY Come girls, let us circulate the bottle.

SOPHY   A very good notion, Cousin, and I will second it with all my heart. Stanly, you don't drink.

STANLY   Madam, I am drinking draughts of love from Chloe's eyes.

SOPHY   That's poor nourishment indeed. Come, drink to her better acquaintance.

The SERVANT *serves the wine.*

MISS FITZGERALD   This, ladies and gentlemen, is some of my dear Grandmother's own manufacture. She excelled in Gooseberry Wine. Pray taste it, Lady Hampton.

LADY HAMPTON (*chokes and splutters*)   How very refreshing!

MISS FITZGERALD   I should think, with your Ladyship's permission, that Sir Arthur might taste a little of it.

LADY HAMPTON   Not for worlds. Sir Arthur never drinks anything so high.

FITZGERALD (*kneeling*)   And now my amiable Sophia, condescend to marry me.

SOPHY (*embracing him*)   I will!

STANLY (*kneeling*)   Oh, Chloe, could I but hope that you would make me blessed!

CHLOE (*embracing him*)   I will!

MISS FITZGERALD   Since you are the only one left, Willoughby, I can no longer refuse your earnest solicitations! *(She pushes* WILLOUGHBY *onto his knees.)* There is my hand!

LADY HAMPTON *(rising)*   And may you all be happy!

ALL   May you all be happy!

As all the GUESTS *rise to join in the toast,* LADY HAMPTON *tips* SIR ARTHUR *onto the floor.*

Music

LOVE AND FRIENDSHIP

Characters

MARIANNE, a young girl
ISABEL, Marianne's mother
LAURA, Isabel's friend
YOUNG LAURA
MOTHER to Laura
FATHER to Laura
EDWARD, husband to Laura
AUGUSTA, Edward's sister
SOPHIA, wife to Augustus
AUGUSTUS, friend to Edward
LORD ST. CLAIR, Laura and Sophia's grandfather
PHILANDER, Lord St. Clair's grandson
GUSTAVUS, Lord St. Clair's second grandson
MACDONALD, Sophia's cousin
JANETTA, Macdonald's daughter
M'KENRIE, Janetta's lover
OLD WOMAN

The action of the play takes place in a variety of locations and moves fluidly from one scene to another. Scene changes are indicated by lighting and sound effects. Furniture is minimal but a sofa stage left and seating for Laura and Marianne downstage right will be helpful.

Scene 1. Bath, 1790

A parlour in a lodging house

MARIANNE, ISABEL *and* LAURA *enter upstage centre.*
LAURA *and* MARIANNE *are carrying baskets and dressing-cases.*

MARIANNE   My dear Mama, I cannot believe we are arrived in Bath at last!

ISABEL   And after a journey almost perfectly free of accident and hardly any dust.

LAURA   Overturned only once! The coach had all the comforts of dirt, litter and little children.

ISABEL   But they were very quiet and of a reasonable size.

MARIANNE   Such comfortable rooms! And in Laura Place!

ISABEL (*grudgingly*)   Up two pairs of stairs. Bath does not answer my expectations. The streets are not as gay as I had hoped. The place is all vapour, shadow, smoke and confusion.

MARIANNE   What a wonderful prospect of balls lies before us!

LAURA   Do not rejoice too soon, Marianne. The temptations Bath may offer are many, even to a young girl of moderate charms, like yourself. And more mature beauties may also attract disagreeable attentions.

ISABEL   How true! My dear friend Laura, I entreat you to tell my daughter of all the misfortunes of your life so that she may be warned of the dangers of the world.

LAURA   No, my friend, not until I am no longer in danger of experiencing such dreadful misadventures.

ISABEL   You are fifty-five today. If a woman is ever to be safe from disagreeable lovers and the cruel persecutions of obstinate fathers, surely it must be at such a time of life.

LAURA   I cannot agree with you, Isabel. Experience has taught me that where charms remain, they are irresistible to evil men.

ISABEL (*searching among the luggage*)   Where is my dressing-case?

LAURA   Although I may once again be exposed to adventures, the afflictions of my past life may prove a useful lesson to you, Marianne.

ISABEL   Learn from them, my Marianne. I must look to our boxes.

ISABEL *exits.*

MARIANNE   I long to hear your story, Ma'am.

LAURA   I will gratify your curiosity, dear Marianne. My
father was a native of Ireland and an inhabitant of
Wales. My mother was the illegitimate daughter of a
Scotch Peer by Laurina, an Italian opera girl. I was
born in Spain and received my education at a
convent in France. When I was eighteen I returned
to my parents in the Vale of Uske. Though my
charms are now somewhat impaired by my
misfortunes, I was once beautiful. My
accomplishments too, begin to fade - I have entirely
forgot the De la Cour Minuet.

Appropriate snatches of music underscore this speech.

MARIANNE   Alas! I believe your minuet was once near
perfect.

LAURA   My dearest friend was your mother. Though
pleasing in her person and manners, between
ourselves she never possessed the hundredth part
of my beauty or accomplishments.

MARIANNE   But she had seen the world! She passed
two years at one of the best boarding schools in
London. She spent a fortnight in Bath and even
dined one night in Southampton.

LAURA   Indeed. I remember how she used to say
'Beware my Laura, beware the insipid vanities and
idle dissipations of the Metropolis. Beware of the
unmeaning luxuries of Bath and the stinking fish of
Southampton'. But Alas! How was I to taste the
dissipations of London, the luxuries of Bath, or the

stinking fish of Southampton? I, who seemed doomed to waste my youth and beauty in a humble cottage in the Vale of Uske.

MARIANNE   A cottage in the Vale of Uske? How horrid!

LAURA *leads* MARIANNE *to a seat.*

Music and a lighting change indicate a flashback to LAURA's *early life.*

Scene 2. Laura's home in the Vale of Uske

YOUNG LAURA *and her* FATHER *and* MOTHER *enter upstage left and sit on the sofa. Her* FATHER *reads a Bible and her* MOTHER *sews.*

LAURA   One evening in December we were greatly astonished to hear a violent knocking on the door of our rustic Cot.

Loud knocking.

FATHER   What noise is that?

MOTHER   It sounds like a loud rapping at the door.

YOUNG LAURA   It does indeed.

FATHER   I am of your opinion. It certainly appears to proceed from violence exerted against our unoffending door.

YOUNG LAURA   Yes! It must be somebody who knocks for admittance.

FATHER *(pedantically)*   We must not try to determine on what motive the person may knock - though I am partly convinced that someone does rap at the door.

Loud knocking continues.

MOTHER   The servants are out. Had we not better go and see who it is?

YOUNG LAURA *(eagerly)*   I think we should.

FATHER   Certainly, by all means.

MOTHER   Shall we go now?

FATHER   The sooner the better.

YOUNG LAURA *(anxiously)*   Oh! Let no time be lost!

The knocking grows louder.

MOTHER *and* FATHER *both remain calm, while* YOUNG LAURA *becomes increasingly agitated.*

MOTHER   I am certain there is somebody knocking at the door.

FATHER   I think there must be.

YOUNG LAURA   At last! The servants are returned. I hear Mary going to the door.

YOUNG LAURA *listens at the door.*

YOUNG LAURA   A young gentleman is at the door! He has lost his way! He is very cold and begs leave to warm himself by the fire. Oh, won't you admit him?

FATHER   You have no objection, my dear?

MOTHER   None in the world.

EDWARD, *a fashionable and romantic young man, enters upstage centre.*

YOUNG LAURA (*aside*)   A young gentleman! The most beauteous and amiable youth that I have ever seen! I feel sure the happiness of my future life must depend on him!

EDWARD   My name is Edward. I am the son of a Baronet, and my mother is dead. I do have a sister of the middle size. My father is a mean and mercenary wretch - it is only to such particular friends as yourselves that I would betray his failings. Seduced by the false glare of fortune and the deluding pomp of title, he insisted on my marrying the Lady Dorothea.

YOUNG LAURA   No! Never!

EDWARD   I said 'Lady Dorothea is lovely and engaging, but know Sir, that I scorn to marry her. No! Never shall it be said that I obliged my father!'

YOUNG LAURA   I admire the noble manliness of your reply!

EDWARD   I mounted my horse and set forth for my sister's house. My father's house is situated in Bedfordshire, my sister's in Middlesex, and though I flatter myself with being tolerably proficient in geography, I found myself entering this beautiful vale, which I find is in South Wales. It was now perfectly dark, but I discerned a distant light. Impelled by fear, cold and hunger, I begged admittance.

YOUNG LAURA   It was freely granted, dear Sir.

EDWARD   And now my adorable Laura, when may I hope to receive the reward of all my painful sufferings? Oh, when will you reward me with yourself?

YOUNG LAURA   This instant, dear and amiable Edward!

They embrace.

FATHER   I will immediately unite you. Though I have never taken orders I have been bred to the Church.

He blesses the happy pair. Wedding music. YOUNG LAURA'S *parents bid* EDWARD *and* YOUNG LAURA *farewell and exit upstage left.*

LAURA   After taking farewell of my parents and my dear friend Isabel, your mother, I accompanied Edward to his sister Augusta's home in Middlesex.

Scene 3. Augusta's home in Middlesex

AUGUSTA *enters and greets* YOUNG LAURA *and* EDWARD *formally.*

LAURA   Edward's sister, Augusta, who was indeed of the middle size, was there when we arrived. She received me with a disagreeable coldness and forbidding reserve. I soon perceived that she was one of those inferior beings who lack delicate feeling, tender sentiments and refined sensibility. Although I had know her more than half an hour she confided to me none of her secret thoughts or asked any of mine. Her arms were not opened to receive me to her heart though I attempted to press her to mine.

MARIANNE   How unexpected and distressing!

YOUNG LAURA *retires to the sofa in distress.*

LAURA   I accidentally overheard a conversation between Augusta and Edward, which increased my dislike for her.

AUGUSTA   You must know our father will never be reconciled to this imprudent marriage.

EDWARD   Augusta, how could you imagine that I would consider my father's opinions? Did you ever know me follow his advice since the age of fifteen?

AUGUSTA   Since you were fifteen! My dear brother, ever since you were five! But you may be obliged to degrade yourself by seeking support for your wife in the generosity of our father.

EDWARD   Never, never! What support will my Laura want from him?

AUGUSTA   Only those very insignificant ones of food and drink.

EDWARD   Food and drink! Do you imagine there is no other support for my Laura's exalted spirit than the indelicate employment of eating and drinking?

AUGUSTA   None so efficacious.

EDWARD   And did you never feel the pangs of love, Augusta? Can you not imagine the luxury of living in every distress that poverty can inflict, with the object of your dearest affection?

AUGUSTA   Where did you pick up this gibberish? I suspect you have been reading novels.

EDWARD   I scorn to answer you. It would be beneath my dignity.

AUGUSTA   You are too ridiculous to argue with. But wait! I hear our father's carriage approaching!

AUGUSTA *exits.*

EDWARD   Sir Edward comes to reproach me for my marriage to Laura. But I glory in the act. It is my greatest boast that I have incurred the displeasure of my father! Come away, Laura!

YOUNG LAURA   But where, my Edward?

EDWARD   My father's carriage is at the door - let us take it and drive to the estate of Augustus, my most intimate friend, which is but a few miles distant. We will be warmly welcomed by my dear Augustus and Sophia his wife.

Scene 4. The home of Sophia and Augustus

SOPHIA *enters.*

SOPHIA   Edward! My husband's dearest friend! You must be Laura! Let us exchange vows of eternal friendship!

YOUNG LAURA   Let us unfold to each other the most inward secrets of our hearts!

AUGUSTUS *enters.*

EDWARD   Augustus! My life! My soul!

AUGUSTUS   Edward! My adorable angel!

EDWARD *and* AUGUSTUS *fly into each other's arms.* SOPHIA *and* LAURA *faint on the sofa.*

AUGUSTUS   You must consider our house as your home.

EDWARD *and* YOUNG LAURA (*together*)   We will never leave you!

AUGUSTUS   My dear loves!

SOPHIA   My dear friends!

MARIANNE   What happiness!

LAURA   But alas! Such happiness was too perfect to be lasting. The marriage of Augustus and Sophia had been contrary to the inclinations of their cruel and mercenary parents.

MARIANNE   But how had they lived? I trust they had independent means?

LAURA   Alas, no. On their marriage, Augustus had gracefully removed a considerable sum of money from his unworthy father's desk. But they scorned to reflect on their poverty and would have blushed at the idea of paying their debts. And what was their reward! The beautiful Augustus was arrested and taken to Newgate Prison and we were informed that we would shortly be evicted.

MARIANNE   Alas! What did you do?

LAURA   What could we do! We sighed and fainted on the sofa.

SOPHIA *and* YOUNG LAURA *faint.*

LAURA   Edward went with his friend to Newgate. We waited for his return. But no Edward appeared. This was too cruel a blow - we could not support it, we could only faint.

AUGUSTUS *and* EDWARD *exit.* SOPHIA *and* YOUNG LAURA *faint again.*

MARIANNE But why did you not go to your parents in the Vale of Uske?

LAURA You may perhaps have been somewhat surprised, my dearest Marianne, that I should not have informed you of a trifling circumstance - the death of my parents a few weeks after my departure.

MARIANNE An orphan! Alone in the world! But my mother would have received you gladly.

LAURA You forget that unfortunately she had married your father and removed to a distant part of Ireland.

MARIANNE My dear birthplace! I pray that I shall never see it again! But what did you do next?

LAURA At length I arose and dragged Sophia to the carriage and we instantly set out. I ordered the postilion to drive to Newgate.

SOPHIA Oh, no, no! I cannot go to Newgate! I shall not be able to support the sight of my Augustus in so cruel a confinement. To behold it would overpower my sensibility.

YOUNG LAURA But where shall we go?

SOPHIA Laura, I have a relation in Scotland, Macdonald, who will not hesitate to receive us. When we change horses at the next inn, I will write an elegant note to Macdonald, informing him of our melancholy situation.

Scene 5. The Inn Yard

YOUNG LAURA Look, Sophia! A carriage is entering the inn-yard. Somehow an instinct tells me that the elderly gentleman descending from it is my grandfather. (LORD ST. CLAIR *enters and she embraces him.*) Grandfather! I beg you to acknowledge me as your grandchild.

LORD ST. CLAIR Acknowledge thee! Yes, dear resemblance of my Laurina and Laurina's daughter, sweet image of my Claudia and my Claudia's mother, I do acknowledge thee as the daughter of the one and the granddaughter of the other.

SOPHIA The instinct of Nature whispers to me that we are in some degree related - but whether grandfathers, or grandmothers, I cannot determine.

LORD ST. CLAIR What is this? Another granddaughter! Yes, yes, I see you are the daughter of my Laurina's eldest girl.

PHILANDER *enters and embraces* LORD ST. CLAIR.

LORD ST. CLAIR Another grandchild! What unexpected happiness to discover in the space of three minutes, as many of my descendants! This I am certain is Philander the son of my Laurina's third girl, the amiable Bertha. We need only the presence of Gustavus to complete the union of my Laurina's grandchildren.

GUSTAVUS, *another young man, enters.*

GUSTAVUS   And here he is! I am Gustavus, the son of Agatha, your Laurina's youngest daughter. *(He embraces* LORD ST. CLAIR.*)*

LORD ST. CLAIR   I see you are, indeed. But tell me, have I any other grandchildren in the house?

GUSTAVUS   None, my Lord.

LORD ST. CLAIR   Then I will provide for you all without further delay. Here are four banknotes of £50 each. Take them and remember I have done the duty of a grandfather.

LORD ST. CLAIR *exits.*

SOPHIA   Ignoble Grand-sire!

YOUNG LAURA   Unworthy grandfather!

SOPHIA *and* YOUNG LAURA *faint in each other's arms.* PHILANDER *and* GUSTAVUS *steal their banknotes and sneak out.*

SOPHIA *(coming to her senses)*   Where are Gustavus and Philander? And where are the banknotes?

SOPHIA *and* YOUNG LAURA *faint again.*

SOPHIA   My cousin, Macdonald!

MACDONALD *enters.*

MACDONALD   Cousin Sophia, welcome to you and your fair friend. My daughter Janetta depends on you both returning with me to Macdonald-Hall.

MACDONALD, SOPHIA *and* YOUNG LAURA *exit.*

Scene 6. Macdonald Hall

LAURA   To Macdonald Hall we went, and were received with great kindness by Janetta.

MARIANNE   Janetta! What a beautiful name? And what was she like?

LAURA   She was only fifteen, and tolerably well-looking. Unfortunately her father had prevailed on her to accept an offer of marriage from a young man called Graham.

YOUNG LAURA, SOPHIA *and* JANETTA *enter.*

SOPHIA   Janetta, I am convinced that Graham has no soul. He has never read the *Sorrows of Werther*, and his hair has not the least resemblance to auburn.

YOUNG LAURA   Surely you can feel no affection for him. The fact of his being your father's choice ought to be a sufficient reason for rejecting him.

SOPHIA   Janetta, it is impossible that you could love Graham. It is your duty to disobey your Father.

JANETTA   But I know of no other young man for whom I have the smallest affection.

SOPHIA   Such a thing is impossible!

JANETTA (*shyly*)   I believe I do like Captain M'Kenrie better than any one else.

YOUNG LAURA   I believe you are violently in love with him!

SOPHIA   Has he ever declared his affection for you? Did he never gaze on you with admiration - tenderly press your hand - drop an involuntary tear - and leave the room abruptly?

JANETTA   Never - he has never left particularly abruptly or without making a bow.

YOUNG LAURA   Indeed it is absolutely impossible that he should ever have left you without confusion and despair. We will acquaint him of your feelings by an anonymous letter.

SOPHIA (*writing*)   'Oh! happy lover of the beautiful Janetta, why do you delay a confession of your attachment? A secret marriage will at once secure your happiness. A friend.'

SOPHIA *gives the letter to* M'KENRIE, *who is waiting at the door.* M'KENRIE *enters.*

M'KENRIE   Amiable Janetta! Modesty had been the only reason for concealing the violence of my affection for you! If you will have me, let us fly to Gretna Green, and there celebrate our nuptials. (*They embrace.*)

M'KENRIE *and* JANETTA *exit.*

SOPHIA My dear Laura, I happened to open a private drawer in Macdonald's library with one of my own keys. I discovered some bank notes of considerable value. Look!

YOUNG LAURA It would be a proper treatment of so vile a wretch as Macdonald to deprive him of his money.

As SOPHIA *and* YOUNG LAURA *count the money* MACDONALD *enters.*

MACDONALD What is this, Madam? Do you mean to defraud me of my money?

SOPHIA Wretch! How dare you accuse me!

MACDONALD This is ignoble behaviour, madam! A fine repayment for the hospitality you have enjoyed at my expense.

YOUNG LAURA Base Miscreant! How can you sully the spotless reputation of Sophia's bright excellence? Why do you not suspect my innocence as well?

MACDONALD Be satisfied Madam. I do suspect it. I desire that you both leave this house at once.

SOPHIA Nothing but our friendship for Janetta could have induced us to remain so long beneath your roof, despicable man!

YOUNG LAURA   Janetta has fled to Gretna Green but two hours since with her adored M'Kenrie. By this act of friendship to Janetta, we have amply discharged every obligation to you.

MACDONALD   You have thrown her into the arms of an unprincipled fortune hunter. Leave my house this instant!

SOPHIA *and* YOUNG LAURA *exit, followed by* MACDONALD.

Scene 7. The Turnpike Road

MARIANNE   Alas! Where did you go?

LAURA   We left Macdonald Hall, and after about a mile we sat down by the side of a clear limpid stream. A grove of full-grown elms sheltered us. Before us ran the murmuring brook and behind us ran the turnpike road.

Country sounds, birdsong, etc.

YOUNG LAURA   What a lovely scene! Why are not Edward and Augustus here to enjoy its beauties with us?

SOPHIA   Ah! for pity's sake do not remind me of my imprisoned husband. I cannot bear to hear him mentioned - it affects me too deeply.

YOUNG LAURA   Excuse me, Sophia, for having offended you. Instead, let us admire the noble grandeur of the elms.

SOPHIA   Alas! my Laura, do not wound my sensibility. Those elms remind me of Augustus. He was like them, tall, majestic - he possessed that same noble grandeur. (*Pause*) Why do you not speak, my Laura? Do not leave me to my own reflections.

YOUNG LAURA   What a beautiful blue sky!

SOPHIA   Oh! Laura, do not distress me by calling my attention to an object which so cruelly reminds me of my Augustus's blue satin waistcoat!

A carriage approaches; there is the sound of the carriage overturning, shrieks, etc. EDWARD *and* AUGUSTUS *are flung on stage.*

YOUNG LAURA   A carriage! Alas! It has overturned!

SOPHIA   Look! Two gentlemen have been flung into the road! I observe they are elegantly attired but alas! They are weltering in their blood!

YOUNG LAURA   Oh Heavens! Look! It is Edward and Augustus! Dead!

SOPHIA (*shrieks*)   My Augustus!

YOUNG LAURA   My Edward!

SOPHIA *and* YOUNG LAURA *collapse in hysterics.*

MARIANNE   Alas! How unfortunate! How did you bear such a dreadful loss?

LAURA   Sophia shrieked and fainted, I screamed and

58

instantly ran mad. (YOUNG LAURA *demonstrates, raving and shrieking.*) We continued for an hour and a quarter - Sophia fainting every moment and I running mad. At length we heard a groan from the hapless Edward.

YOUNG LAURA   He yet lives! He breathes!

EDWARD *groans.*

SOPHIA   Alas! Do not die!

YOUNG LAURA   Do not die, my Edward!

EDWARD (*weakly*)   Laura, I fear I have been overturned.

YOUNG LAURA   Oh! Tell me Edward, tell me before you die, what has befallen you since we were separated?

EDWARD   I will…

EDWARD *dies.* SOPHIA *faints and* YOUNG LAURA *runs mad.*

MARIANNE   Dead indeed! What did you do?

LAURA   Sophia sank again into a swoon. My grief was more audible. My voice faltered, my eyes assumed a vacant stare, my face grew as pale as death.

YOUNG LAURA (*raving*)   Give me a violin. I'll play to him and sooth him in his melancholy hours— Beware ye gentle nymphs of Cupid's thunderbolts, avoid the piercing shafts of Jupiter—Look at that grove of trees—I see a leg of mutton—They told me Edward was not dead; but they deceived me—they took him for a cucumber.

MARIANNE   How piteous. How long were your senses impaired?

LAURA   For two hours I raved madly and was not in the least fatigued.

YOUNG LAURA *continues to rave. Finally,* SOPHIA *revives.*

SOPHIA (*shaking her*)   My Laura, I entreat you to return to your senses. Consider that night is now approaching and the damps begin to fall.

YOUNG LAURA   But whither shall we go?

SOPHIA   To yonder white cottage.

YOUNG LAURA   Let us knock and ask for shelter.

Scene 8. The White Cottage

An OLD WOMAN *appears.*

SOPHIA   Can you give us a night's lodging?

OLD WOMAN   My house is but small, I have two bedrooms, but you are welcome to one of them. I am a widow with one daughter, who is just seventeen.

The OLD WOMAN *exits.*

MARIANNE   The best of ages! I am also just seventeen. What was she like?

LAURA   She was very plain and her name was Bridget. Therefore she could not be expected to possess exalted ideas, delicate feelings or refined sensibilities. She was nothing more than a good-tempered, civil and obliging young woman.

MARIANNE   As such you could scarcely dislike her.

LAURA   No, indeed. She was only an object of contempt. Ah! What were the misfortunes I had before experienced to those which now occurred! The death of my father and mother and husband were trifles in comparison. The next morning, Sophia complained of a violent pain, and a disagreeable headache.

SOPHIA *(coughs)*   Alas, I have caught a cold by my faintings in the open air as the dew was falling.

YOUNG LAURA   I believe I have escaped the same indisposition. My fits of frenzy so effectually warmed my blood as to make me proof against the chilling damps of night. I fear that it will be fatal to you, my Sophia.

SOPHIA *lies down on the sofa.* YOUNG LAURA *kneels beside her, holding her hand.*

LAURA   Alas! my fears were justified. Her disorder turned to a galloping consumption. However, I received some consolation in the reflection of my having paid every attention to her in her illness. I had wept over her every day, bathed her sweet face with my tears and pressed her fair hands continually in mine.

MARIANNE   Kind attentions, indeed!

SOPHIA (*expiring*)   My beloved Laura, take warning from my unhappy end. Beware of fainting-fits. Though they may be refreshing, they will prove destructive to your constitution - run mad as often as you choose; but do not faint...

YOUNG LAURA   I will ever heed your dying advice, dear Sophia.

MARIANNE   I too will always remember her tragic end and her words of warning.

SOPHIA *exits.*

Scene 9. The Stagecoach

LAURA   After attending my lamented friend to her early grave, I immediately left that detested village. I was soon overtaken by a stagecoach, in which I instantly took a place.

SIR EDWARD, AUGUSTA, PHILANDER *and* GUSTAVUS *enter and arrange themselves as if in a stagecoach.*

SIR EDWARD *snores loudly.*

YOUNG LAURA   How dark it is! I cannot see my
    fellow travellers. What an illiterate villain that man
    must be! What a total want of delicate refinement!
    But wait! It is Sir Edward, the father of my lost
    husband! And by his side his daughter Augusta.
    And my cousins Philander and Gustavus! All the
    nearest connections of my dead Edward!

AUGUSTA *(waking up)*   What is that you say? Is my
    brother dead? What has become of him?

YOUNG LAURA   Yes, that luckless swain your
    brother, is no more!

AUGUSTA   Alas! Tell us the whole melancholy affair.

LAURA   I related to them every misfortune that had
    befallen me. *(She speaks very quickly.)* The
    imprisonment of Augustus and the absence of
    Edward—our arrival in Scotland—our unexpected
    meeting with our grand-father and our cousins—
    our visit to Macdonald-Hall—the service we
    performed for Janetta— her father's inhuman
    behaviour—our lamentations on the loss of
    Edward and Augustus—and finally the melancholy
    death of my beloved Sophia.

This passage is underscored by appropriate music.

AUGUSTA   What a sad tale of misadventure!

AUGUSTA *and* SIR EDWARD *exit.*

Scene 10. The Inn

LAURA   When we arrived at the next inn, while the rest of the party was devouring green tea and buttered toast, my cousins Gustavus and Philander related to me everything that had befallen them in their lives.

MARIANNE   Oh, let me hear their adventures!

PHILANDER   We are the sons of the two youngest daughters which Lord St. Clair had by Laurina, an Italian opera girl.

GUSTAVUS   Our mothers could neither of them exactly ascertain who were our fathers.

PHILANDER   It's of little consequence as our mothers were certainly never married to either of them.

GUSTAVUS   It reflects no dishonour on our blood, which is of a most ancient and unpolluted kind.

PHILANDER   Our mothers' united fortunes had originally amounted to nine thousand pounds, but it had diminished to nine hundred.

GUSTAVUS   This nine hundred pounds they kept in a drawer in our sitting parlour. When we had reached our 15th year, we took the money and ran away.

PHILANDER   We were determined to manage our prize with economy. We divided it into nine portions, the first of which we devoted to food -

GUSTAVUS   - the second to drink -

PHILANDER - the third to housekeeping -

GUSTAVUS - the fourth to carriages -

PHILANDER - the fifth to horses -

GUSTAVUS - the sixth to servants -

PHILANDER - the seventh to amusements -

GUSTAVUS - the eighth to clothes -

PHILANDER - and the ninth to silver buckles.

GUSTAVUS We hastened to London and had the good luck to spend our money in seven weeks and a day which was six days sooner than we had intended.

PHILANDER We accidentally heard that both our mothers had starved to death, and determined to engage ourselves to some strolling company of players, as we had always a turn for the stage.

GUSTAVUS We offered our services to one and were accepted; our company was indeed rather small, as it consisted only of the Manager, his wife and ourselves.

PHILANDER Our most admired performance was Macbeth. The Manager always played Banquo, his wife Lady Macbeth. I did the Three Witches and Philander acted all the rest.

(as a Witch) 'By the pricking of my thumbs, something wicked this way comes.'

GUSTAVUS *(as Macbeth)* 'How now, you secret, black and midnight hags, what is't you do?'

PHILANDER *(as another Witch)* 'A deed without a name.' And having acted all over England, and Wales, we came to Scotland.

GUSTAVUS We arrived in that very town where you met your grandfather. We were in the inn-yard when his carriage entered and knowing that Lord St. Clair was our grandfather we decided to get something from him by revealing the relationship.

PHILANDER You know how well it succeeded, but you bear us no rancour, I trust. Having obtained the two hundred pounds, we left our Manager and his wife to act Macbeth by themselves, and took the road to Sterling, where we spent our little fortune to great effect.

YOUNG LAURA Amiable youths, I wish you all good fortune and happiness.

They embrace and PHILANDER *and* GUSTAVUS *exit.* AUGUSTA *enters.*

AUGUSTA Madam, as the widow of his son Edward, my father desires that you accept four hundred pounds a year from him.

YOUNG LAURA Little reward for my devotion to his memory! But inform Sir Edward that I accept his offer.

AUGUSTA *exits.*

Scene 11. The Lodging house in Bath

LAURA   And that is my story, Marianne. I hope you have learned to honour the claims of true sensibility against the demands of ungrateful and ungenerous parents.

MARIANNE   Indeed. And what of the others involved in your misfortunes?

LAURA   Augusta is united to Graham, Janetta's lover. He abandoned her when she was disinherited by Macdonald. My father-in-law, Sir Edward, married Lady Dorothea, my Edward's intended, in hopes of gaining an heir. His wishes have been answered.

MARIANNE   And those charming young men, your cousins?

LAURA   Philander and Gustavus went to Covent Garden, where they still perform under the names of Lewis and Quick.

MARIANNE   How very satisfactory!

LAURA   And as you know, I retired to a romantic village in the Highlands of Scotland where I could indulge in a melancholy solitude uninterrupted by unmeaning visits. And then you and your mother somehow discovered me.

MARIANNE   What happiness! I often recall that
   touching encounter.

ISABEL *enters, carrying her dressing-case.*

ISABEL   It was there at last we found you!

LAURA   And there you received once more the
   unfortunate Laura to your bosom!

LAURA *and* ISABEL *embrace.*

ISABEL   Alas! When we had parted in the Vale of Uske,
you were still united to the best of Edwards. You had
then a father and a mother –

LAURA   And I had never known misfortune.

ISABEL   I still delight to reflect on the happy chance
   that brought us to your door. Having lost my
   husband in Ireland – I know not how – I
   determined to relieve our grief through the healing
   powers of Nature. Encountering Sir Edward on the
   Stagecoach between Edinburgh and Sterling, he
   told us of your sad situation.

MARIANNE   How could we abandon you, my
   mother's oldest friend, in that desolate spot? What a
   happy thought it was to unite our resources and
   remove here to Bath! I have always longed to see
   this place of dissipation.

ISABEL   It took us but a moment's reflection. With your £400 and the remnants of my Irish property, I knew we could make quite a presence in this city – renowned for surface and appearance as it is.

LAURA   Although our charms may be somewhat impaired, yet I believe that by taking the waters, I, at least, may repair much of my former beauty.

MARIANNE   And let us try to remember the De La Cour minuet!

They attempt to dance an increasingly awkward minuet.

THE PLAYS IN CONTEXT

Austen's early writings became generally available for the first time in 1922 when an edition of *Volume the Second* of the *Juvenilia* was published. All three of her notebooks have since appeared in various editions.

The inspiration for the plays in this book comes from the essentially dialogic quality of Austen's early writings and the majority of the situations, characters and dialogue in each play have been taken directly from the originals. Alterations and omissions have been made only where necessary to provide dramatic shape. Reading and performing these adaptations of her delightful early works will make them easily accessible and should encourage a new generation of readers to enjoy the *Juvenilia*.

Both *The Three Sisters* and *The Visit* come from *Volume the First* of Jane Austen's *Juvenilia*, which is held in the Bodleian Library, Oxford.

THE THREE SISTERS

The Three Sisters was dedicated to Jane's older brother Edward, who had been adopted by the wealthy Knight family and was about to marry a baronet's daughter.

This unfinished novel, written as a series of letters, clearly shows the harsh economic necessity that was the driving force behind many marriages of the time. It is very difficult to make exact comparisons but the genteel Mrs Stanhope and her three daughters are living on an income of £500 a year, equal to about £20,000 today. Mary's suitor, Mr Watts, has a large annual income of £3000 - about £120,000 today. This is a great inducement to marriage, at least from Mrs Stanhope's point of view. The personal allowance - 'pin-money' - that Mrs Stanhope demands for her daughter would amount to about £8,000 today.

After the death of their father in 1805, Jane, her sister Cassandra and their mother discovered what genteel poverty was like. Such families were dependent on their wealthier relations and Jane Austen's brothers did their best to help their mother and sisters, each contributing £50 a year. Mrs Austen and Cassandra had capital producing about £200 annually but Jane had nothing. When she was twenty-seven years old she accepted an offer of marriage from an eligible and financially desirable suitor but immediately changed her mind and broke off the engagement the following day.

Jane Austen often touches on women's difficult financial circumstances in her novels. Both *Sense and Sensibility* and *Persuasion* show families in similar difficulties after the death of the father. In most cases, unless girls married well, the outlook was bleak. As Jane put it in a letter to her sister Cassandra, '*Single women have a dreadful propensity for being poor, which is one very strong argument in favour of matrimony*'.

Other options for girls in such circumstances were extremely limited. Like Jane Fairfax in *Emma*, well-born girls might find a position as a governess or companion or even teach in one of the schools for young ladies that were becoming popular. Many girls had to accept such a fate. Without money, there was little freedom for women whether they were married or not.

In this adaptation of *The Three Sisters*, some of the detail in the novel has been omitted and an ending has been added using some of Austen's words from elsewhere.

THE VISIT

The Visit is one of several short plays included in the *Juvenilia*. Family theatricals were popular in the Austen household and were encouraged by the Rector and his wife. At holiday time the young people of the family and their friends put on some quite ambitious plays, including Sheridan's *The Rivals* in 1784 and Fielding's burlesque *Tom Thumb* in 1787. Jane's brother James, eleven years her elder, was very involved in these theatricals, writing witty prologues and epilogues.

The plays were performed in the barn, which was fitted up as a theatre for the occasion. In *The Three Sisters*, one of Mary's many demands is that her suitor should build her

> *a theatre to act plays in. The first play we have shall be 'Which is the Man', and I will do Lady Bell Bloomer.*

Mrs Cowley's play *Which is the Man* was the Austens' Christmas play at Steventon in 1787. Even as a teenager, Jane was well acquainted with the rules and conventions of the theatre from these family performances and from her extensive reading. To parody a genre successfully it is necessary to know it very well.

While apparently conforming to the conventions of the time, *The Visit* is actually quite subversive. The gentlemen sit on the laps of the ladies and at least one of the ladies proposes to a gentleman. Jane Austen has fun devising a particularly unappetizing menu. The dishes seem rather coarse food for an elegant if unusual dinner party. Liver and crow is a dish of pig's liver and chicken giblets, and tripe is the boiled stomach lining of a cow. Fried cowheel and suet pudding are equally unrefined. A red herring, an expression used to mean something that is a distraction or a false clue, is actually a kipper, sometimes used to train hounds when hunting. All these dishes would be familiar to poor families but it is extremely unlikely that such food would ever appear on the tables of the gentry.

Austen's nephew James Edward Leigh-Austen notes in his *Memoir* that, when his aunt was young, '*beer* and homemade wines, especially mead, were more largely consumed'. A large quantity of alcohol is consumed during this unusual meal and even a young lady like Sophy is happy to 'toss off a bumper', although the unfortunate Sir Arthur is never allowed by his wife to have anything to eat or drink. The young Jane Austen clearly found drunkenness amusing and many of the characters in her early stories are overly fond of food and drink.

In *Evelyn* from *Volume the Third* of the *Juvenilia*, Mr. Gower is offered a light snack before dinner.

> *The chocolate, the sandwiches, the jellies, the cakes, the ice and the soup soon made their appearance, and Mr. Gower, having tasted something of all and pocketed the rest, was conducted into the dining parlour where he made a most excellent dinner and partook of the most excellent wines.*

In *Jack and Alice* from *Volume the First* of the *Juvenilia*, we learn of the Johnson family who, although '*a little addicted to the bottle and the dice, had many good qualities*'. Later in the story, after '*an elegant and well managed entertainment the whole party were carried home, dead drunk*'.

Were such scenes familiar to the teenage Jane Austen? It is interesting that in a letter to her sister Cassandra in 1800, when she was twenty-five, Austen writes

> *I believe I drank too much wine last night... I know not how else to account for the shaking of my hand today. You will kindly makes allowances...*

LOVE AND FRIENDSHIP

This epistolary novel was written in 1790 when Jane Austen was in her fifteenth year. *Love and Freindship* (sic) was dedicated to her cousin, the lively and fashionable Madame La Comtesse de Feuillide.

Eliza de Feuillide was the most exotic of the Austen relations. Born in India, she married a French aristocrat who was guillotined in 1794 during the French Revolution. She had known Jane's older brother Henry since he was a teenager, and after her husband's death she married him. Eliza de Feuillide enjoyed performing in several of the Steventon theatricals when Jane was a young girl.

Love and Freindship is written as a series of letters from Laura to her friend Isabel's daughter, Marianne. In recounting her story to Marianne, Laura reveals her egotism, her vanity, her disregard for conventional morality and her lack of sincere feeling. These characteristics are only surpassed by the selfishness and criminality of her friend Sophia. Laura claims that her only fault is

> *a sensibility too alive to every affliction of my Freinds, my Acquaintances, and particularly to every affliction of my own.*

Both Laura and Sophia are given to fainting at every crisis in their fortunes. Jane Austen anticipated this affectation in *Frederick and Elfrida*, the first piece in *Volume the First* of the *Juvenilia*, where the heroine

76

was in such a hurry to have a succession of fainting fits, that she had scarcely patience enough to recover from one before she fell into another.

Austen was familiar with such heroines from her favourite novel, *Sir Charles Grandison* by Samuel Richardson, and from Sheridan's comedy *The Critic*, which satirizes the absurdity of many of the stage conventions of the day. In fact, she borrowed a number of other elements from *The Critic*. As well as the fainting, the following extract from Act III Scene 1 is obviously the model for the recognition scene between Lord St. Clair and his grandchildren.

JUSTICE   What is thy name?

*SON   My name's Tom Jenkins, alias have I none -
Though orphaned and without a friend!*

MOTHER   How loudly nature whispers to my heart. Had he no other name?

JUSTICE   No orphan nor without a friend art thou - I am thy father; here's thy mother; there thy uncle, and those are all your near relations!

MOTHER   Of ecstasy of bliss!

SON   O most unlooked for happiness!

JUSTICE   O wonderful event!

(They faint alternately in each other's arms.)

The passage, later in *Love and Freindship*, where

Laura and Sophia faint and run mad on the discovery of their dying husbands also echoes the behaviour of the heroine of *The Critic*, Tilburnia, who *'enters stark mad in white satin'*.

> *TILBURNIA   The wind whistles — the moon rises — see, they have killed my squirrel in his cage! Is this a grasshopper? — No, it is my Whiskerandos — you shall not keep him — I know you have him in your pocket — An oyster may be crossed in love! Who says a whale's a bird?*

Love and Freindship may also be intended as a parody of *Laura and Augustus*, a popular sentimental novel in three volumes of the time. Both novels are told in a series of letters and feature a heroine called Laura and a hero called Augustus and both have heroines who faint and run mad. But Austen exaggerates the misfortunes of her characters to increase the comic effect and instead of three volumes she compresses her story into thirty-five pages.

All the heartless young people in *Love and Freindship* oppose their families' wishes, engage in illicit marriages, squander their money, steal from their parents and each other and excuse their activities by the claims of 'sensibility' or expediency. There are deaths from starvation, illness and accident, but the characters are too selfish to be touched by the misfortunes or physical disasters of others. In this absurd comedy, Austen mocks the conventions of contemporary fiction - love at first sight, the charms of poverty, intense friendships after a moment's acquaintance and high-flown sentiments.

Love and Freindship is the first work in *Volume the Second* of Austen's *Juvenilia*. The original is held in the British Library.

PRODUCTION NOTES

These three plays may be performed as a full evening's entertainment. Alternatively, each play may be presented separately.

Staging

The plays can be adapted to any performance space but will work most effectively in very simple settings. The more flexible and imaginative the staging, the more interesting the result will be.

A minimum of furniture should be used. If all three plays are presented, most of the same furniture can be used for each of them. A chaise longue or sofa downstage left and chairs downstage right will be sufficient for *The Three Sisters* and *Love and Friendship*. Six chairs and a circular or rectangular table will provide the setting for *The Visit*. If necessary, the food and drink in *The Visit* can be mimed and even the presence of a table is not essential. A simple circle of chairs will make the actors more visible to the audience. Three entrances — upstage right and left and centre stage — will allow characters to come and go easily.

With ten scenes, *Love and Friendship* is the most complex of the plays in terms of its settings but it is not necessary to attempt to recreate these multiple locations.

The action should flow smoothly and the entrances and exits of the characters can occur as Laura narrates the story to Marianne. The setting up of each scene will work best when incorporated into the action.

Lighting changes will indicate the various scenes and help to create mood and atmosphere. Laura's narration and appropriate sound effects will signify each new setting, for example the noise of the inn yard and events such as the overturning of the stagecoach.

Music

Introducing the performance with period music, either live or recorded, will help to set the atmosphere and an appropriate song or a piece of music linking each of the plays will enhance the experience. It will also allow the actors time to set the scene for the next play. The use of music to underscore some of the key moments – Laura's 'wedding' or Sophia's death – will be very effective and one or more live musicians on stage would be an added bonus.

The University of Southampton has digitized 600 pieces of music, including popular songs of the time, from the Austen family albums and these are now available online.

Costume

Authentic Regency costume, if available, will add to the production values. If the actors are playing more than one role, any costumes that are too complicated are likely to present problems. Alternatively, the women might wear long dark skirts and tops and add scarves, bonnets, aprons or shawls to differentiate the characters. The men might wear dark trousers and shirts or jackets or cloaks. If actors are 'doubling' several roles, try to define each role by simple changes or additions to their costumes, perhaps by adding scarves, hats or cloaks.

Cast

It should be possible to present all three plays effectively with a cast of eight actors. *The Three Sisters* has a cast of four women and one man. *The Visit* needs four women and four men. There is also the non-speaking role of the servant. Because of the essentially absurd nature of the plays, there is nothing to prevent gender or age-blind casting. In *Love and Friendship,* for example, two women might play the roles of Gustavus and Philander.

Eighteen different characters are listed in *Love and Friendship*, but with doubling the play could be presented with seven or eight actors. For example, the actor playing Laura's Father could also play Lord St. Clair, and the actor playing Isabel could also double as several other female characters. Where the number of female performers is limited, the roles of Laura and Young Laura may be played by the same actor, with Laura entering and leaving each scene as she narrates her adventures to Marianne.

Cast for *Love and Friendship* with eight actors:

Female Actor 1 - Marianne
Female Actor 2 - Isabel/Laura's Mother/Augusta/Old
Woman/Janetta
Female Actor 3 - Laura/Young Laura
Female Actor 4 - Sophia
Male Actor 1- Laura's Father/Lord St. Clair/M'Kenrie
Male Actor 2 - Edward/Philander
Male Actor 3 - Augustus/Gustavus
Male Actor 4 - Macdonald/Sir Edward

BIBLIOGRAPHY

Many editions of Jane Austen's six novels are available. Original publication dates:

1811	*Sense and Sensibility*
1813	*Pride and Prejudice*
1814	*Mansfield Park*
1816	*Emma*
1817	*Northanger Abbey*
1818	*Persuasion*

Juvenilia

Austen, J. *Volume the First.* (Oxford, 2013)

Austen, J. *Volume the Second.* (New York, 2014)

Austen, J. *Volume the Third.* (New York, 2014)

Select Bibliography

Austen, J. *Juvenilia & Early Works.* (Cambridge, 2013)

Austen-Leigh, J. E. *A Memoir of Jane Austen by her Nephew.* ed. R.W. Chapman (Oxford, 1926)

Baker, W. *Critical Companion to Jane Austen: A Literary Reference to Her Life and Work.* (New York, 2008)

Austen, J. *Catherine and Other Writings,* eds. Doody, M.A. and D. Moore (Oxford, 1993)

Harman, C. *Jane's Fame: How Jane Austen Conquered the World.* (London, 2010)

Hughes-Hallett, P. ed. *'My Dear Cassandra'. Jane Austen: Letters to her Sister.* (London, 1991)

Le Faye, D. ed. *Jane Austen's Letters.* (Oxford, 1995)

Southam, B. ed. *Jane Austen's Sir Charles Grandison.* (Oxford, 1980)

Tomalin, C. *Jane Austen: A Life.* (London, 1998)

Todd, J. *Jane Austen: Her Life, Her Times, Her Novels.* (London, 2013)